F
My Father's
Religion

Mohamad Faridi

Destination-USA, Inc
P.O. Box 50007
Colorado Springs, CO 80949

Graphic Design: Spencer Everett

First Edition Published: 2016
Second Edition (Revised): 2025

This book is dedicated to my wife, Susan, and my supporting Pastors, Glen and Janice Lambert, who encouraged me to put my testimony into writing. A big thank you to Jerry Churchill and his family, who made the publishing of this book possible.

Prologue

I was 21 years old, a devout Muslim on the outside, but hollow on the inside. The rituals of Islam, once sacred and comforting, had become empty motions. The endless rules, the fear of punishment, the pressure to be perfect all left me numb and hopeless. I was ready to give up on life.

I was told a million times, that Islam was the 'straight path', the only way to truth, but it had led me only to an empty abyss. "If this isn't it, then what is?" It was then that Jesus came, not through a dream or vision, but through the words of a friend. His words pierced through the deception I was operating under—the belief that I had to hurt myself, shed my blood, and sacrifice my life for eternal life. The veil of Islam that had blinded me from the truth was torn, and I could finally see.

This is the story of how I met Jesus, the Son of the Living God—and how He rescued me from the crushing weight of a diabolic religion and gave me freedom, purpose, and a brand-new life.

My Father's Religion

I was born in 1984, five years after the succession of the Islamic Revolution, raised in a devout Shi'ite family in Tehran, Iran, during a brutal war between Iran and Iraq that would come to define my entire generation. The Shi'ites were fighting the Sunnis, both slaughtering one another in the name of Allah, believing that spilling blood would earn them Paradise. I was born in 1984, right in the middle of the Iran-Iraq War, an eight-year bloodbath that devoured thousands of lives.

Our generation was called *"the generation of war,"* and for a good reason. The Iraqi jets roared in the skies, rockets and bombs rained from above. The walls of our home trembled as if they, too, were afraid. The windows were taped in an X-shape to keep the glass from shattering into our home. I was just a toddler when my mother gathered me into her lap, pulling her veil over me as if that thin layer of fabric could shield me from the chaos outside.

The sounds of sirens, war anthems, and lamentations were my lullaby. This war wasn't just political or military; it was religious. The leader of Iran, Ayatollah Khomeini, declared: *"The sacrifices of war are what keep Islam alive."* As a family, we lived out these words.

My Uncle, my father's brother, volunteered to join the war, defending Islam and his country; he died a martyr, leaving behind his wife and four kids. His body was never returned to our family, only the news of his death. The title of *Shaheed*, the greatest honor bestowed upon a Muslim, was given to him; and his sacrifice was celebrated. The street my grandparents lived on was renamed in our family's last name, and his mural was painted on the wall of the largest mosque in the neighborhood.

The Shaping of a Child Soldier

The war ended, but its grip on us never loosened. Even as a child, I was raised with the culture of war, martyrdom, and Jihad. The war of being a good Muslim will never be over. My generation had to be ready. The battlefield might change, but the fight for Islam had to continue.

At school, we were taught about a 13-year-old boy, *Mohammad Hossein Fahmideh,* who had become the hero of our nation. When Iraqi tanks rolled into his city, he took grenades from the bodies of dead soldiers, strapped them to himself, and threw himself in front of an advancing tank, blowing himself up to stop the invasion. He was the idol of our time. His face was on banners, and his name was sung in anthems. I wanted to be like him.

We were children, but we weren't raised as children. We were raised as soldiers. When I attended the mosque in our neighborhood, it wasn't just for prayer. After the congregational prayers and the cleric's sermon, we were lined up—row after row of boys—like a miniature army. The *Basij* began their drills. They taught us how to march in formation and how to obey without hesitation. Even the sound of rockets was simulated. When the whistle of an incoming missile was played through speakers, we were trained to drop, to cover our heads, to brace for impact—as if the battlefield was already ours. The message was clear: you are not here to dream or play. You are here to fight, if necessary, to die.

At school, before we ever stepped into our classrooms, the day began with the Quran. A student would stand before the entire student body and loudly recite a passage. After that, the physical training began. We were young boys doing jumping jacks and stretches in the schoolyard—but as we counted, it wasn't "one, two, three" like other children around the world. It was: "One, two, three—death to America. One, two, three—death to Israel." These chants were instilled in us as naturally as learning math or grammar.

Almost every floor hallway from the yard to the classrooms was painted with the flags of the "enemies" of Islam—the United States and Israel. And before we could enter our classes, we were ordered to walk over them, to stomp on them. It was part of our routine. We couldn't avoid it or question it. We just followed orders. We weren't being taught how to think, we were being taught who to hate.

For field trips, our school would take us to museums of war, with graphic and gruesome exhibits and images of wounded and dead soldiers. These things etched something into my soul.

The world of Islam that I was born into dictated everything— who I was, what I was called, how I lived, and the very measure of my worth. "Islam is the best," they said. "The most complete religion. The straight path. We had to be thankful every day to Allah for choosing us. We are Muslims *Alhamdulillah*, chosen for a destiny." I wanted to be a good Muslim; I committed myself to the disciplines of Islam. I prayed five times a day. Before dawn, I would wash myself with cold water and stand on my prayer rug facing the direction of the city of Mecca, repeating Arabic prayers I was taught to memorize. Even though my mother tongue is Farsi, the language of the Persians, I was told that Allah only accepts prayers in Arabic.

I remember asking my mother one day, "Mom, we're Iranians; we speak Farsi. Why do I need to speak Arabic to God?"

She looked at me sharply as if the very question was dangerous. "A good Muslim doesn't ask questions," she replied. "Islam means surrender. A good Muslim simply surrenders." Then she quoted the Quran, Chapter 5, verse 101 and explained it to me, "If matters have been made clear to us, we don't need to ask questions. If you ask questions, my son, it leads to doubt. Doubt leads to sin, and Allah will burn sinners, doubters, and overthinkers in Hell." And so, I did surrender because I was frightened.

That was the answer to my childlike curiosity. Questions lead to doubt, doubt leads to sin, and Allah will burn sinners in hellfire forever.

The Example

My mom was the perfect Muslim woman. She never missed a prayer and constantly recited the Quran under her breath. The Quran recitation or Arabic Islamic prayers were always playing on an old radio in the background. She was the upholding pillar of Islam in our home. The one teaching the tenants of faith and the one who held us accountable.

Islam made my mom very superstitious. She always had on her veil, careful not to expose even a strand of hair to any man outside what Islam prescribed. Everything in our home was about what is Halal and what is Haram. What is permitted and what is not permitted. What is clean and what is unclean. She did ablution over and over again, sometimes for things that made no sense to me—almost like she believed an invisible, an unseen impurity could separate her from Allah's Paradise for eternity. Her faith didn't give her peace. It made her paranoid, always second-guessing, religiously obsessive.

One thing that always unsettled me more than anything else was that when my mother was with her husband and children, she could remove her veil. But when she stood before Allah in prayers, she had to be fully covered. I couldn't understand it. Was Allah offended by the sight of her hair? Was her hair dangerous? Was Allah, who created her body in perfect detail, now repulsed by what he himself had made?

It made no sense to me. In Islam, we were told that a woman's hair is *awrah*—something private, something shameful to expose in front of others. But how could it be shameful before her Creator? Why did Allah, who supposedly knows her more intimately than anyone, require her to cover her hair during prayer? Were we, her husband and sons, somehow more familiar or trusted than Allah?

During my childhood, I watched her carefully pin down every strand, smoothing the scarf tight against her forehead before each prayer. If even one hair escaped, she would start over. It wasn't a matter of modesty anymore; it was fear. Fear that her prayer wouldn't be accepted. Fear that Allah would reject her for something as small as a glimpse of hair.

That fear shaped her being. The veil was no longer just a covering; it was a symbol of distance. The very act of coming to Allah for your ritualistic prayers required hiding. Even in the most intimate spiritual moments, Allah remained distant, veiled from her, and she from him.

My mom had specific Arabic phrases from the Quran memorized for every situation. She was always chanting, repeating these phrases over and over; her rosary was constantly moving between her fingers. *Bismillah,* in the name of Allah, was the word she said most. Everything had to be done *in the name of Allah*—from the smallest action to the biggest decision. This was a superstitious attempt to protect herself and us from unseen dangers that she was bothered by.

When we needed to make decisions—a purchase, work, travel, or even small daily choices—we didn't weigh options or pray for wisdom. We performed *istikhārah*. An Islamic way of knowing what to do. My mother would often turn to the Quran, open it at random and read the first verse on the right-hand page, convinced it held a message from Allah. Entire Islamic books categorized these verses into answers like excellent, good, average, or very bad—not based on the context of the verse, but on long-held traditions or God knows what. It was less revelation and more spiritual roulette.

And if the Quran wasn't used, the *tasbih* beads were. My mother would whisper her Arabic chants, grab a handful of beads with her left hand, and count them two by two until only one or two were left. One bead meant "do it." Two meant "don't." I remember watching her hands move, breath held tight in my chest, waiting to see if we were allowed to move forward or not. Sometimes, the result could determine the direction of our lives. It felt sacred. It felt serious. But it wasn't peace; it was pressure.

The Fear of Hell

Hell was not an abstract concept to me. It was real, as real as the streets I walked on. From the time I was young, I was taught about the horrors that awaited those who displease Allah.

Islam has stories of respected scholars who died and came back to warn us—men who had memorized the Quran, went to Mecca for pilgrimage, those who had prayed and fasted, who died and were still punished in the grave. Their sins, though small, had not been forgiven, and so they faced the torture of the afterlife. I heard these stories constantly. I listened to them on cassette tapes, or at the neighborhood mosque sermons. I attended to them, trying to understand what I had to do to avoid the same fate.

In my sleep, night after night, I screamed desperately for help. No one could hear me. Trapped in my terrors, I saw Islam's afterlife—the *Sirat Bridge*, that narrow, razor-thin path stretched over Hell, the path every Muslim must walk on to get to the other side for safety. There was no way around it. Everyone was falling, swallowed by eternal damnation. I would wake up in the middle of the night; my body covered in cold sweat from the nightmares. Darkness was present in my room, and there was no escape from it.

I didn't want to be one of those who fell into the abyss. I didn't want to burn in Hell.

Living Under the Law

Islam dictated everything: how to pray, how to sleep, where to sleep, how to eat, how to wash, what direction to face during prayer, what to wear, and a million other rules. Every part of my life was controlled by Islamic law. I spent hours each day studying and obsessing over those rules, afraid of breaking even one. A single mistake could bring severe consequences.

And when I broke the law, which happened many times. I knew the cost. The sin was weaponized. Allah held the sin's guilt over my head and threatened me with hellfire and torture of the grave.

In Shi'a Islam, we believed in penance—paying for our sins with voluntary self-punishment inflicted as an outward expression of repentance for having done wrong. That was what we had been taught—that pain purifies, that blood is the price of redemption. So, we harmed and mutilated our physical bodies in a ceremonial way to make guilt disappear.

During the month of Muharram, the month of blood, we mourned the Imams who had sacrificed their lives for Islam. But our mourning wasn't just in words, we mourned with our bodies. We cried out, wailed in anguish, and self-flagellated, physically manifesting our grief. Through this, we deeply connected with and identified ourselves with the suffering and deaths of those who were the mediums between men and Allah.

During the first ten days of Muharram, we gathered together every evening to perform these rituals. The clerics would recite the stories of lamentations; the mournful sound of it filled the air, setting the tone of sorrow. The men would beat their chests with their hands at the rhythm of the songs of the eulogy. I joined them, pounding my chest until it was bruised. But that was just the beginning. At other ceremonies, barefoot on hot asphalt roads, we carried chain whips, striking our backs for hours on end until they were raw with blood.

I saw grown Muslim men crawl on the streets like snakes— dragging their faces and bodies across the dirt as they approached a shrine. They believed such a sacred place demanded that level of humiliation and worthlessness to the degree that they didn't believe they even deserved to walk upright. They moved like worms, wailing while crawling, hoping their display of self-loathing would earn them something. To them, the path to holiness was paved with shame.

But then, there were those of us who went even further to express devotion.

We would imitate the violent death of one of the most loved saints, Imam Ali, by striking swords on our own heads. Through this reenactment of his suffering, we identified ourselves with his death, devotion, and sacrifice for Allah. The first time I performed this ritual, I knelt before the *Mullah* with my heart pounding. He chanted the name of Imam Ali repeatedly while wiping the sword clean of the blood from the person he had struck before me. He raised the sword high, and when he struck me, I heard the strikes inside my head. With each strike the cold steel sliced through my scalp, causing a sharp pain followed by a warm rush of blood. When the strikes were over, I stepped back, touched my head, and looked at my hand—chopped hair mingled with blood.

I was paying for my sins, trying to rid myself of the condemnation that came with it. But no matter how much I harmed my body or devoted myself to Islam and its ways, no matter how much I tried, the guilt never left. Deep down, I knew it wasn't enough—I wasn't enough. Allah always demanded more.

Never Enough

No matter how much I did, no matter how much I prayed, it was never enough.

I began to wonder—how much more did I have to suffer? How much more blood had to be shed? How much more did I have to do to measure to have assurance that Allah had accepted me?

I traveled to northeast Iran on a pilgrimage, hoping to find that something I was missing. At the shrine of the eighth Imam, I prostrated myself—lying flat, face down, my nose and forehead pressed against the marble flooring—praying, desperately seeking answers from Allah, anything. While I was there, I sought out the scholars, the ones who had separated themselves from the world and devoted their entire lives to the teachings of Islam. After much searching, I found a highly respected cleric. I made an appointment and waited for hours to speak with him. I had high hopes that he might have my answers. Finally, when I was face-to-face with him, I listed for him all I have done and then I asked the question that had haunted me for years, "What else do I need to do to be certain that I will be accepted by God?"

He looked at me and said, "Son, there is still much to do. You have not done enough. Islam is much deeper than you think." I asked, "Do you think you have done enough? Are you certain of your afterlife?" He answered, "No one is."

Instead of answers, his words caused a deep sense of hopelessness to settle over me. I walked away with more questions. If even the most devout Islamic scholars couldn't be sure of their place with Allah, what chance did I have? How many more prayers, how many more pilgrimages would it take? How much more self-loathing and punishment of my body? And how much more self-inflicted pain?

I was doing everything to please Allah; to prove I was an obedient Muslim. But no matter how much I did, my prayers were met with silence. The transcendent was too holy, too distant, and too far above someone like me.

Military Service

After finishing high school, being a male and healthy, I was ready to serve my country in my mandatory army duty. I was assigned to the Revolutionary Guard of Iran, a religious army—not a choice of mine, but what Allah's fate had decided for me. I was sent to the midland deserts of Iran for boot camp. It was in that place that we were trained to submit to authority, to march in unison, and to dedicate ourselves to a larger cause as we were molded into soldiers of Islam.

When I returned from boot camp, the army sent us on a trip called *Rahian-e Noor*, which means 'The Path of Light.' We rode buses from Tehran to southwest Iran, near the Iraq border, where some of the bloodiest battles of the Iran-Iraq War had taken place. It was the same region where my uncle and two of my cousins had died as martyrs about twenty years earlier.

The trip was meant to remind us of their sacrifices. They told us we were walking the same ground as the martyrs and that it was our duty to carry the spirit of jihad, martyrdom, and self-denial. They filled our heads with stories of bravery and bloodshed, and made it clear that we were part of a bigger mission. Something worth dying for.

Facing the Fear of the Grave

As part of this spiritual journey, at night they took us to a massive graveyard filled with empty tombs. The commemoration of the martyrs was part of this worship, and the leaders of this ritual told us what it would take to be great. One by one, they placed us into those empty graves to confront the fear of death.

"This is how you reunite your spirit with the spirit of martyrdom, with the spirit of Jihad," they said. After I laid in the deep grave, the shadow of darkness around me was tangibly heavy. I could feel the narrow walls closing in, and for a moment, I thought I might be buried alive there. It was a terrifying experience. If I held my hand in front of my face, I couldn't see it; it was that dark. We were being prepared to face death without fear, to not be afraid of the grave, and to be ready to give our lives for the cause of Islam.

The deeper I got into Islam, the darker it was. Was there any way out of this wretched, hopeless trap that held me captive?

Encountering the Truth

A Good Friend

Right after finishing my military service, I came back home, trying to figure out what was next. What should I do with my life now? Everything felt uncertain. Maybe if I reconnected with some old friends from high school, I could see how they were navigating life. One of them was Rasoul. We had known each other since we were six, his mom and my dad were both lab technicians at the same hospital.

Rasoul was just three days older than me—tall and skinny—and came from a devout Muslim family like mine. Over the years, we sometimes ended up in the same school. But when it came time for military conscription, Rasoul was medically exempt. Because of my own service, we didn't see each other for two full years.

One day, I called him up, and he said, "Mohamad, let's get together. It's been a while."

I had a motorcycle, and I went and picked him up. We rode to a quarter in northeastern Tehran, a former village, and a summit on the slopes of the Alborz Mountain. As we chatted to get caught up, within ten or fifteen minutes, I could tell something about him was different. He was the guy who in school was hot-tempered, always looking for trouble. But now, he was calm. Too calm. There was a peace about him that seemed fabricated, and honestly, it bothered me. So, I pressed him, "What's wrong with you today? What happened to you?"

He physically was the same and looked the same, but he wasn't the same person anymore. I pressed him more, "Tell me, what is the reason for your change?" He answered, "I've become Christian."

I couldn't believe what I was hearing. My eyes got big! A Muslim doesn't just *become* Christian. I have never heard of such a thing. That's not how it works. Why would someone go and convert to a lesser religion? We, Muslims, have been proudly taught our whole life that Islam is the perfect religion, superior to all other religions, and every other religion is corrupted. On top of that, one of the articles of Islam is fate—everything is preordained by Allah. You are born a Muslim, you live a Muslim, and you will die a Muslim. There is no other way. How could you alter the destination Allah has for you? I was madly confused by that one statement.

Our conversation got heated fast. With everything in me, I argued with him, trying to correct him, to set him straight. I quoted the Quran and challenged his decision, but nothing I said seemed to shake him. No matter how hard I pushed, he stayed steady and peaceful.

Finally, after a couple of hours of back-and-forth, Rasoul looked me in the eye and said, "Mohamad, you asked me why I've changed. I'm telling you; it's Jesus."

Jesus Did What I Couldn't Do

"The last thing I share with you is this, and after that, I need to get going. It's getting late." He continued, "Jesus was sacrificed for you. He was beaten. He was bruised. He was cut. His precious blood was shed for your sake. He was crucified, and He gave up His life. He sacrificed His Life for you, and if you believe this and receive it, you could know God and have eternal life."

When I heard that, the veil of deception of Islam, which I had lived under for almost 22 years, was torn. Now I could see. A light switched on inside of me. I had spent my entire life beating myself, bruising myself, cutting myself. I had shed my own blood, thinking I would impress God. I was ready to do anything as a Muslim, even to sacrifice my life if necessary, hoping that maybe, just maybe, it would be enough. But the result of the worship of Allah and following the teachings of his prophet was nothing other than uncertainty and misery.

What Rasoul shared was the best thing I have ever heard. It wasn't just words—it was something much more profound, something that cut straight through me. It felt like a sword had pierced my heart, exposing the wickedness inside. In that moment, I stood naked before a holy God, empty-handed, with nothing to offer Him.

Rasoul said, "Mohamad, it's already finished." Everything as a Muslim I was trying to do has already been done in the person of Jesus Christ. And if I only believed, I would have eternal life. That is the good news. That's the one, best thing I have ever heard in all of my life. Jesus' sacrifice was accepted, and mine was utterly useless. The work of redemption was done. I was settling a debt to God that was already settled by His Son and well accepted.

That was the moment the Word of God entered my heart; I realized all my striving had been in vain. The war was over. I was fighting a war that was already won. I had spent my whole life trying to earn what had already been freely given. I just didn't know about it. For the first time I heard the Gospel, the truth therein shattered every lie I had believed.

I dropped to my knees, literally dropped. I looked up at Rasoul and begged him, "What do I need to do? Tell me, what do I need to do to have what you have?"

"Close your eyes," he said. He led me in a simple prayer— repenting of my sins, surrendering to Jesus as my Savior and Lord, humbly receiving what He has done for me. I repeated every word after him. I believed it with all my heart.

And the second I opened my eyes after this prayer, I saw colors for the first time. Everything became vibrant. Things around me suddenly were lively. I just knew something significant had happened. Something had changed.

"Rasoul, what's going on?" I asked. "What is happening to me?"

He smiled and said, "Mohamad, Jesus came into your life. And it's the best thing that could ever happen to you."

At that moment, the physical weight I had carried my entire life—the crushing burden of trying to please God, of striving to do enough, of living in fear—was gone. It was like someone had reached inside of me and ripped that thing out. The war was over!

For once, I felt free.

My Faith Crisis

After Rasoul left that day, I headed home alone. I was enjoying the fresh air I was able to breathe. But then the reality of what had just happened began to settle in, and two questions started to weigh on my mind. First, if Jesus had truly died for us all, why wasn't I told sooner? Why isn't everyone who knows this reality, shouting it from the rooftops? How could something so life-changing, so freeing, be hidden? Second, if Christ and Christianity were true—then Islam must be false. That thought shook me. Could everything I had been taught, everything my family believed in, everything our society was built on, be a lie? Was the foundation of my entire world based on a false ideology? How could that be?

My heart was overwhelmed with profound peace, but my mind was in conflict. I was facing a great crisis, a faith crisis. So, I went on a journey to resolve it.

First Church Experience

That same week, Rasoul reached out and invited me to visit a church with him. In Tehran, there were a few old churches, cathedral-like buildings that resembled museums more than places of worship. But they weren't for us. They belonged to the Armenian community, Christians by birth, and were closed off to Muslims.

Growing up, I was taught that churches were off-limits—foreign, suspicious, even spiritually contaminated. The mullahs often repeated things like, "Christians eat pork and live in immorality. That makes them unclean." In school and sermons, I heard hadiths like this one from Imam Sadiq: "God forbade pork because it dulls a man's sense of honor, corrupts his morals, and leads to shamelessness. It even causes incest or murder." That kind of teaching shaped how I viewed non-Muslims—not just as different, but as defiled. To step into a Christian Church wasn't just a matter of religious difference. It felt, in my mind, like stepping into impurity.

So, when Rasoul invited me to go to a church, I didn't know what to make of it. Everything I knew about the Church and the Christians was negative. People like us didn't just walk into churches. We didn't belong there. Even though I accepted Christ earlier that week, I had so much against the Church.

On the other hand, it wasn't as if the Armenian Christians simply welcomed Muslims into their churches with open arms.

And honestly, who could blame them? For centuries, they had lived as second-class citizens under Islamic rule—tolerated but always watched. Their churches were destroyed for random reasons, their communities threatened, and their rights restricted. In Iran, it is illegal for Christians to share their faith with Muslims. Under the Sharia law, the foundation of the Islamic Republic's legal system, evangelism is considered a crime. To do so could bring government punishment or worse.

Generations of persecution had taught the Christians of the Middle East to be cautious, especially around Muslims. Even if someone like me came with a genuine interest, how could they know I wasn't a spy? How could they trust that I wasn't going to report them to the authorities for allowing me in their midst? Their guardedness wasn't for no reason. They had learned the hard way that safety meant keeping outsiders out.

However, there are always a few who refuse to compromise and bow to fear. These are the ones who believe God's law stands above the laws of men. One of them was an Armenian taxi driver who shared the Gospel with Rasoul's aunt during a simple cab ride. That small act of courage didn't end there. It planted a seed that grew. Rasoul's aunt eventually became a Christian, and she went on to share the truth with her nephew. That's how I heard it.

It was a Friday morning when Rasoul and I arrived at the church at least an hour before the service. Thanks to our connection in the Armenian community, we were able to pass through security and were let in the building. My eyes darted everywhere, taking in every detail.

Then, as Rasoul was saying hi to the people in the front yard of the church, I went ahead to check the place out on my own. Soon after, I found the sanctuary. The doors of the sanctuary were open. I peeked inside, and I couldn't resist going in. The moment I stepped through the oval-shaped gate, an overwhelming sense of God's presence embraced me. It felt like being wrapped in a cloud of peace—so magnificent, yet so tender. The tangible presence of a holy God was washing over me. At that moment, I heard a voice within me, clear and undeniable: "You're home. You're home." The words brought a deep sense of peace to my soul. Had I completed my journey of finding God? Did I finally arrive? Could this be the place I was always looking for?

I was completely immersed in God's presence, savoring every moment of it. Lost in the experience, I didn't want anything to interrupt the flow of His love pouring over me. Quietly, I found my way to a pew in the back and sat down, hoping to remain unnoticed—just me and Him, surrounded by the gentle warmth of His love.

I don't know how long I sat there, completely submerged in what I was feeling. Then people started coming in, one by one, filling the pews around me. What jolted me out of my quiet awe was this: men and women were sitting together in the same room. I had never seen anything like that in a place of worship. In the mosque, men always pray in front, while women are behind, hidden by curtains or in separate rooms. But here, they sat side by side as equals. It stunned me. I didn't know what to think. It was beautiful yet very different. And the surprises didn't stop there.

The minister picked up a guitar, slung it over his shoulder, and began to play. A woman at the piano, joining in. Then they started singing—and to my shock, the entire congregation sang along. Some even clapped their hands. I froze. What kind of worship is this? What kind of God is honored like this? My thoughts raced, colliding with everything I had ever known.

In Islam, religious gatherings—no matter the occasion—are filled with lamentations, not music. The clergy's role is to stir grief. If the crowd didn't respond with enough passion or sorrow, the cleric would beat his face and chest to show them how it was done, provoking others to follow. We remembered the suffering of our Imams, their martyrdoms, and the supposed injustices they faced. Worship was expected to be somber, weighty, and full of sorrow. Joy is considered evil in Islam.

However, here, these Christians were smiling, singing, and clapping as if they had something to rejoice in.

I leaned in, trying to catch the words of their songs. I needed to understand the reason behind their joy. Why did Muslims mourn while Christians celebrated?

One song stood out the most:

> *Yes, Jesus, You gave it up for me. You gave up glory, You gave up the splendor. Yes, You gave it up for me. You gave up Your life on the cross. You forgave my sins and gave me hope. Yes, You did it for me. You defeated death and You rose, and Yes, You did it for me.*

The lyrics stunned me. They weren't singing about a prophet or a martyr who simply died and stayed dead. They were singing about a God who gave up everything for them. A God who forgives sin. A God who gives hope. And this wasn't just a tragic ending. They were celebrating because He had risen from the dead. He came back to life!

That changes everything.

In Islam, we mourned our dead leaders because they remained dead. That's why there are so many shrines all around us—to commemorate this truth that they are dead, and here is their remaining. But these Christians weren't clinging to a grave. They were rejoicing in an empty tomb.

This God was different. And so was the worship He desired.

Being shaken by the whole service, I carefully continued my examination. After the sermon ended, the minister prayed in Farsi, not Arabic. That alone was a major shock. Then they called their God, Father. They spoke to Him directly, without facing a specific direction or even without ritual washing. What kind of God listens so personally? This wasn't the god of Islam. This was someone entirely different.

Then, the minister invited everyone to stay for tea and cookies, a time of fellowship. Rasoul and I left the sanctuary and made our way downstairs. The people there were warm, kind, and genuinely welcoming. Before we left, Rasoul stopped at the church's small bookstore and bought me a Farsi New Testament. He looked at me and said, "This is the living Word of God. If you read it, it will change your life. It was written for you."

I couldn't hide my facial expression; I raised an eyebrow and gave him a look. In my mind, I half-laughed, repeating his words with a bit of sarcasm: "The living Word of God... written for me?" It sounded absurd. Everything I knew growing up was that the Bible is corrupted. But I was on a journey to figure Christianity out and resolve my faith crisis.

Wrestling With the Word of God

I took the book home. I knew having a Bible was illegal in Iran. Then, a thought came to mind: "If it's corrupted, why would it be illegal?" If Islam is so perfect and complete, why aren't Muslims allowed to read any religious book other than Islam? That didn't make any sense.

So, I began reading the book. After a few chapters in the Gospel of Matthew, I found myself wrestling with it, captivated by Jesus' teachings in the Sermon on the Mount, chapters 6 and 7. I couldn't put the book down. As I read, it was as if Jesus was personally speaking directly to me, exposing everything as a Muslim I had spent my entire life doing as empty, meaningless, and powerless.

When I reached Matthew 6:5, I felt exposed. Jesus said, "When you pray, do not be like the hypocrites. They love to stand and pray in the synagogues and on the street corners to be seen by others." I had done exactly that, thinking this was the right way. The evening prayers, especially, I prayed not just in private but out in the open—on yards of shrines, in mosques, and even when a guest at someone's home. For the *Juma Salat*, a huge number of us would roll out prayer rugs on streets for all to see, shoulder to shoulder, forming rows, standing, bowing, and prostrating.

But Jesus called it what it was, a show of hypocrisy. He said, "Truly, I tell you, they have their reward." The approval of men was all we would ever get. Jesus' method was the opposite: "But when you pray, go into your room, close the door, and pray to your Father, who is unseen. Then your Father who sees what is done in secret will reward you."

I sat there stunned with my book in my hands. I had spent my entire life making sure people saw my devotion, but I had no assurance that Allah had ever seen me. And yet, Jesus spoke of a God who sees, even in secret. A God who didn't need public displays; He wanted sincerity.

Then I got to Matthew 6:7, and my heart dropped. Jesus said, "And when you pray, do not use vain repetitions as the heathen do. For they think they will be heard for their many words." That single verse captured the very way my mother and I had prayed our whole lives. I had spent years repeating the same memorized phrases in Arabic, a language I didn't even understand. Five times a day, I recited the same chapters of the Quran. Even the way I bowed, knelt, and pressed my forehead to the ground was a routine, just another part of the endless repetition.

Beyond the ritual prayers, there was the constant chanting, the rehearsing, the repetition, and the endless rolling of Islamic prayer beads between my fingers. I whispered the same phrases over and over convinced that if I said them enough times, I would be heard.

But Jesus exposed it all in one sentence: "They think they will be heard for their many words." That described us perfectly. It was true of every Muslim I knew. We were pagans, heathens. We weren't communing with God. We were piling up phrases like tokens on an invisible scale, hoping the sheer quantity would earn us something. We called it worship, but it was an empty heathenistic ritual.

After all those years of repetition, I had never once felt that Allah heard me. There was no reply or response. Only mindless duty. This truth was bothering me, but I continued reading, and

Jesus continued, "Do not be like them, for your Father knows what you need before you ask Him."

"Your Father?" That phrase hit me like a slap. In Islam, calling God "Father" is considered blasphemy. From childhood, I had been taught to reject that idea. Every Muslim recites Surah *Al-Ikhlas* seventeen times a day in ritual prayers, which says: "He neither begets nor is begotten." Qur'an 112:3

That one verse is a direct denial of both the Fatherhood of God and the Sonship of Christ. But now, here was Jesus, speaking of God as a Father—a personal, loving Father who already knows what I need even before I ask.

Then I got to Matthew 6:16, and yet again, Jesus exposed another major Islamic practice: fasting. "When you fast, do not be like the hypocrites with a sad countenance. For they disfigure their faces so that they may appear to others to be fasting." That hit hard. In Islam, fasting is yet another public display. We were taught to act sad, tired, hungry, and worn out as if the suffering of fasting made us more righteous. It wasn't spiritual discipline but a show of piety to others. And again, Jesus, cutting straight through the fluff and calling it what it really was—hypocrisy.

That was me too. During Ramadan, I made sure people saw how much I was suffering. My lips were dry, my energy was drained, and my face showed the sacrifice I was making for Allah. We all did it. Every Muslim wanted to be seen by others.

"But when you fast, anoint your head and wash your face, so that you do not appear to men to be fasting, but to your Father who is in the secret place." Matthew 6:18

It was all connected. Every religious act I had performed, the public prayers, endless repetitions, fasting with a sad face, had one thing in common. They were done to be seen. My devotion had always been hypocritical. But Jesus exposed it all as empty. He wasn't impressed by outward displays or rituals done for the approval of others. True devotion, He said, was something deeper. It was about knowing God personally, intimately, and sincerely.

The things I was reading in that Book were unsettling. The more I read, the more I wrestled. It was as if Jesus had reached across time, exposing every ritual I had spent my life performing. But how? Islam came six centuries after Jesus. How could He so precisely call out our prayers, our fasting, our obsession with public displays of devotion before Islam even existed?

It didn't make sense. The Quran taught that Jesus was just another prophet, yet here He was, speaking with authority that shook me to my core. There were only two possibilities: either this book was divine truth, or it was written after the conception of Islam.

Anger boiled inside me. I slammed the book shut and threw it across the room. I didn't want to read it anymore. But I couldn't escape it. Minutes passed. I sat there, staring at the Book on the floor, as if leaving it there would change what I already knew deep down. I had read the truth, and no matter how much it challenged everything I had believed, I couldn't walk away from it.

So, I picked the book back up. I opened it randomly and landed on chapter 24 of Matthew. Thinking "Maybe I should read it here, maybe it will be less challenging." When I reached verse 11, "Then many false prophets will rise up and deceive many," I yelled at the Book, "Are you saying Muhammad, the prophet of Islam, is false? What are you doing to me?"

I closed the Book again. But I could not resist. I opened the pages once more and kept reading from where I left off the last time in chapter 7.

The more I read the Word of God, the more it washed over me, cleansing me and breaking down the strongholds Islam had built in my mind. The process was painful yet gentle, like pure water flowing through the filth in my soul, washing away the spiritual darkness I had lived in for over two decades.

I kept reading, still wrestling, still trying to make sense of it all. My mind resisted, but my heart was drawn in, pulled toward something very amazing and real.

Then, Matthew 11:28 shows up. "Come to me, all who labor and are heavy laden, and I will give you rest. My yoke is easy, and my burden is light, and you will find rest for your souls."

I stopped. Everything in me stopped. For years, I had labored under the crushing yoke of Islam. It was unbearable. A system of endless rules, rituals, and expectations—one that demanded everything but promised nothing. I had fasted, prayed, beaten my body, and recited words I didn't understand, all in hopes that maybe, just maybe, Allah might notice me, Allah would accept me. But there was never rest, never peace—only more striving and more of the same thing with absolute silence on the other side.

And now, here was Jesus. He wasn't commanding me to do more, or demanding another sacrifice, or requiring me to prove myself. He was simply calling me to come to Him with the promise of rest.

This was it. This was what I had been searching for my whole life, "rest". The very thing I had never known in Islam.

I received that Bible on a Friday, the same day I stepped into a church for the first time. From that Friday to the next, in just one week, I read through the four Gospels five times each. I couldn't pull myself away. I couldn't get enough. It was the Bread of Life feeding me straight from heaven. And it was good food.

Another Church Visit

On my quest for truth and in the midst of my personal faith crisis, I decided to visit another church—this time on the west side of Tehran. Most Christian services in Iran were held on Fridays, since Friday functions like Sunday in the Islamic calendar. The service was scheduled to begin at 6:30 p.m., and I got there just in time.

This congregation was much smaller than the previous one. The minister was in his mid-seventies, with a full head of shiny white hair and a matching beard. I sat closer to the front this time, and directly in front of our row stood a simple wooden cross.

The service began, and after a few worship songs, the minister said he wanted to share a testimony. Then he invited a man named Ali to come forward. Ali? What? That was a Muslim name.

At that point, with my limited understanding of Christianity and everything else, I honestly thought I was one of maybe two or three Muslims who had ever converted. But now, there was someone else. Another former Muslim. Another convert—just like me. And his name was Ali.

The minister brought Ali to the stage, a middle-aged, typical Iranian man who had a scarf wrapped around his neck. As he stepped forward, he slowly unwrapped the cloth and revealed a hole in his throat, the result of advanced throat cancer.

He spoke with a raspy voice, "The doctors gave me just a few weeks to live. They told me to go home, be with my family, and get my affairs in order. There was nothing more they could do."

Ali continued, "I was desperate. I went to the shrines. I begged to be healed. I threw all my money into offertory boxes, hoping for a miracle. But nothing happened. My condition only got worse."

Then his voice changed. "One day, I was going past this church. I saw the cross over the building and thought, 'I've tried everything. I have nothing to lose. Let me try their God.' So, I walked in."

Inside the church, he found a few people and shared his situation. They told him, "Let us pray for you." They gathered around him, laid hands on him, and began to pray.

Ali said, "While they were praying for me, I suddenly saw another hand. The hand reached toward me. There was a hole in it, like a big nail had pierced it. That hand with a hole touched the hole of my throat." After their prayer, he left for home.

He paused and then added, "Days went by. But I wasn't dying like the doctors said. I was getting better. I went back for more tests, and the same doctor said, 'We don't know what happened, but there's no trace of cancer.' I told him, 'You may not know what happened, but I do. It was the hand with the print of a nail.'"

As I sat there listening, I was completely engaged, captivated by every word. I knew Ali's story from my Bible readings. It wasn't just a testimony. It was Scripture coming alive right in front of me.

It was the story of the woman in Mark 5:25–30: "Now a certain woman had a flow of blood for twelve years... She had spent all that she had and was no better but rather grew worse. When she heard about Jesus, she came behind Him... and touched His garment... Immediately, the fountain of her blood was dried up, and she felt in her body that she was healed."

Also, in Mark 16:18, Jesus told His disciples, "They will lay hands on the sick, and the sick will recover."

This wasn't just another religious book. These weren't just ideas or religious theories. It was real. The words in it were real. It happened right in front of me.

I didn't need to hear anything more after that. I don't even remember when the service ended. But once people began to rise from their seats and quietly leave, I made my way to the front of the church. I knelt before the wooden cross at the altar and whispered, "Jesus, you are real. You are alive, and Your Word is true. And I will follow You, even if it means dying for it."

The moment those words left my lips, I heard the voice of the Lord responding, "I have died so that you may live. There is no more dying for you."

Some Things Will Never Be the Same

After coming to faith in Jesus, I knew my life would never be the same. I also knew I had to tell my family. I knew if I denied Jesus before men, He would deny me before His Father. I was afraid, especially of my dad. He was strong, harsh, and often abusive. I had been the zealous one in the family, urging my brothers to be devout Muslims. And now, I no longer followed Islam myself.

At home, the change in me was obvious. I no longer practiced Islamic rituals. I stopped going to the mosque. I distanced myself from old friends. I tried to keep it quiet, but Islam is a visible religion. The prayers are done in public. The routines are seen. The language of devotion is spoken out loud. By not doing those things, I was making a statement, even if I did not intend to. My mother was noticing, and it troubled her.

On top of that, I had committed THE unforgivable sin of *Shirk*, saying or accepting that there is another God other than Allah.

One day, I was alone in my room, praying to Jesus the way He taught—quietly, in secret. The lights were off. There was no noise, no rug, no direction to face. Just me, speaking to Him. Suddenly, my father walked in. Suspicion had already been boiling in the house. My parents could sense that something had changed, and they were trying to catch me in the act.

He looked at me with suspicion and asked, "What are you doing?"

I didn't have much choice but to respond. If you knew my dad, avoiding him or deflecting wasn't a thing. I said, "I'm praying."

He looked confused. I wasn't facing Mecca. There was no prayer rug, no familiar posture. It was clear to him that I wasn't following the Islamic routine.

"Who are you praying to?" he asked.

"Jesus, dad." I answered.

He stared at me with rage. Then he asked, "Why Jesus?" and "Why not Muhammad?" At that moment, I thought I was being logical, at least in my own mind, "Dad, Muhammad is dead. How can a dead person hear my prayer?" As soon as I said that my father exploded. He cursed at me and attacked me physically. I pulled away and ran from our home. That incident was the beginning of my persecution from my family.

After several nights of sleeping on people's rooftops and in their doorways, getting bitten by mosquitoes and crawling cockroaches, I was miserable. I didn't know what to do, so I called Rasoul—the friend who had put me into all of this. I explained what had happened, the danger of going back home, and how I had nowhere to go. He told me that at the beginning of his own conversion, his family reacted the same way. But over time, they all have come around and are believers in Christ, and things have changed. He said I could come stay with them until things settled down on my side.

I did that and went to Rasoul's home. Anything was better than my current situation. His entire family were Christians, former Muslims who had surrendered their lives to Jesus. They received me with open arms. In the middle of rejection, when I had no place in my own biological family, God had already prepared another family for me, of His own. Rasoul's family welcomed me, sheltered me, and loved me much better than my own ever had.

Being there, I soon realized I wasn't just staying at a friend's house. I had stepped into the Church of God, into an actual underground church. Rasoul's family regularly hosted visitors, believers just like me. Other Iranians who had once been Muslims, now following Christ. And there weren't just a few. There were many. Some even came from other cities, traveling quietly and cautiously just to gather with other Christians.

That's when it hit me. I wasn't the second or third ex-Muslim Christian. There were a whole bunch of us. I wasn't alone. God was doing something far greater than I had imagined—right there, under the surface of the tyranny of the Islamic Republic.

For the two months I lived there, I didn't realize it at the time—but I was being shaped into a disciple of Christ. We prayed together, took communion. We read the Bible side by side. Many days, we fasted, not just to abstain from food but to serve others. We would take the meals we skipped and give them to the poor. We watched Christian programs on satellite TV and spent hours discussing the Word of God together.

The network of believers I knew was rapidly growing. Christians would visit from cities like Tabriz, Isfahan, Shiraz, and many more. They came with powerful testimonies, and each one left me in awe of God's goodness. I saw how many Iranians, people from all walks of life, were being saved. The sick, the addicted, the sexually abused, the homeless... Jesus was rescuing Iran, one soul at a time.

My travels began with a hunger to see, with my own eyes, what God was doing in other cities and to learn from believers who knew suffering for Christ in ways far more tangible than my own. One of the home church pastors told me the government paid him a visit regularly with threats. He even joked that he had a "regular spot" in prison. He had been beaten and tortured more than once to stop preaching the Gospel or hosting Bible studies.

But he looked at me with calm conviction and said, "I serve a higher government and answer to His laws." Then he quoted 2 Corinthians 4:17, "For our light affliction, which is but for a moment, is working for us a far more exceeding and eternal weight of glory."

The believers in the Iranian underground Church have a contagious boldness—but it came at a great price. I remember one congregation that had received its final warning from the Islamic court: if they met again as Christians, they would all be executed. But they brought that written order, laid it in the center of the room, and worshiped Jesus anyway.

For the next three years, I lived in constant danger while actively serving in the underground church inside Iran. By day, I worked as a taxi driver—but that was just my cover and a way to provide for myself. My real mission was evangelism. I kept my Bible on the dashboard, visible for anyone to see. Whenever a passenger asked about it, I saw it as an open door. I would tell them, "This book is God's love story to you," and then share how He had rescued me from the gloomy life I once lived.

During this time, I was actively spreading the Gospel in every way I could. I distributed hundreds of Bibles across Iran. I made copies of the Jesus Film in Farsi, burning CDs and DVDs late into the night. Then I'd hand them out discreetly or slip them into mailboxes, stairwells, or hidden corners where curious eyes might find them. Every disc, every Bible was planting a seed, one that could take root and change a life forever.

One time, one of my passengers was a veiled woman, which is a sign of strict religious conservatism in Iran. She sat quietly for most of the ride, saying nothing. But just as we reached her destination, as she was about to step out of the car, she paused, pointed to the book on my dashboard, and asked, "What is that book?"

I hesitated for a moment, but I answered honestly, "It's the Bible."

She looked at me and asked quietly, "Can I have one?"

I froze. That day, I had already given away all the extra Bibles I usually kept in the trunk of my car. The only one left was my personal Bible—the one I had wrestled with in the beginning, the one I read every day. The one Rasoul bought for me. I paused for a moment, thinking about what it meant to let it go. But then I got over myself and said, "Sure. You can have it."

I handed it to her. She took it and stepped out of the car without another word. I never saw her again.

Two years later, I was in another country, facing one of the most difficult situations of my life, when my phone rang. I answered. A woman's voice came through: "Mr. Faridi, you don't know who I am. I'm calling to thank you for what you did for us. I was once one of your passengers. I asked about the Bible on your dashboard, and you kindly gave it to me. I read it and I believed its message. I shared it with my husband. He read it and he believed. We talked to both sides of our family, and they came to faith in Christ too. Our parents, my sisters, my brothers... even many of our cousins have accepted the good news. So many more have come to Jesus. I don't want to overwhelm you with details, I just called to say thank you. Thank you for giving me that Bible. It changed my life. It changed my family's life."

Tears filled my eyes. In that dark season of my own life, that one phone call lit a fire in my heart. It reminded me that no labor in the Lord is ever in vain. God was at work, far beyond anything I could see.

Marked By the State

In 2008, the persecution of Christians in Iran took a sharp and dangerous turn. President Ahmadinejad, alarmed by the growing number of Muslim converts to Christianity, addressed the Iranian parliament directly. He testified, "The Christians are stealing the Muslim soldiers from the camp of Islam. We must deal with this issue harshly and with vigilance, or it will grow into something far worse." That day, Evangelical Christianity was officially labeled a national threat to the Islamic regime.

What followed was a wave of mass arrests. Many believers I personally knew were taken—some arrested, some kidnapped, and others simply disappeared. We all understood the terrifying reality; if one person in the underground network was compromised, the entire body was at risk. Under the brutal weight of torture, even the strongest could be forced to talk.

I knew the authorities were hunting me as a traitor because of my activities. The entire network of believers I was connected to had been completely compromised.

One evening, I was returning to the office of the taxi agency I worked for. As usual, I slowed down as I passed by to glance inside—it had become a habit. But what I saw that night wasn't the norm.

Inside the office stood two very tall men in black uniforms. They looked like special forces—intimidating, clearly not your average visitors. They were speaking with the receptionist on duty that night, who happened to be the owner's son.

My heart dropped. Without thinking, I turned off my headlights and killed the engine. Letting the car roll quietly in neutral, I slipped into a parking spot and kept myself hidden in the shadows. I knew something wasn't right.

I waited, watching the office door through my rearview mirror until they finally left. Then, cautiously, I walked in. The owner's son looked pale and shaken. As soon as he saw me, he blurted out, "Faridi… what are you involved in? Those people were asking for you."

He didn't explain who "they" were. But in Iran, when someone says "they," everyone understands—it means the Islamic regime's attack dogs. The owner's son said, "Go home. My dad will talk to you in the morning." I left the office feeling very scared.

The next day, when I arrived at work, I had a feeling something was about to go horribly wrong. As I pulled into the street near the office, the owner spotted my car and hurried outside. Before I could even park, he pointed at me and got into the car. "Drive," he said. I didn't ask any questions. I just started driving.

After a few silent moments, he turned toward me and said, "Faridi, you're like a son to me. The Islamic regime's intelligence is looking for you. They know what you are doing, the people have reported you already! If they catch you, they won't just hurt you. They'll hurt your family too. Do you understand that?"

I felt the weight of his words settle on me like a stone. This wasn't just about my choices anymore. My entire family was now in danger. I was already a point of shame for them because of my conversion; I didn't want to hurt them anymore.

At that point, I reminded myself of Jesus' words: "When they persecute you in one city, flee to another." My first thought was to leave Tehran and find safety in another city. The only people I could trust were fellow Christians I knew in other places. So, I started reaching out to them. But they warned me, "It's dangerous times brother. Please don't even come around here, we already have enough problems. The churches have been attacked, and many have been arrested." I realized I was next on the list, and I knew if I stayed, I would end up in prison. It was time to leave Iran altogether.

Over the course of a few days, I made my decision, gathered what I could, and packed everything I owned into a single duffle bag. The night before I left, I told my family that I had to leave the country because it was no longer safe for me. They thought I was crazy anyway, but they didn't believe I was really leaving forever.

The next morning, I left behind everything I knew and owned, bought a bus ticket to Turkey, and left.

SECTION THREE

Wilderness

The crossing of the Iran-Turkey border was filled with anxiety. I was genuinely afraid that my name might be on a blacklist and that I would be arrested. The bus arrived at the border around midnight. Before we got off, the driver informed us that the bus was having mechanical issues and that we would need to board a different bus after passing through customs on the other side. I gathered my belongings and got off the bus, proceeding to Iranian customs. I cleared customs miraculously without any difficulty but carefully looked back over my shoulders to see if I was being followed, as I walked through a gate into the no-man's land between the two countries. After about twenty yards, I passed through another gate and entered Turkey. There, for the second time, I stood in line with many other Iranians to clear Turkish customs. Around 2:00 a.m., I was finally allowed to proceed to the bus station to catch the Turkish bus to Istanbul. It was a cold morning. Finally, the bus arrived around 5:00 a.m., and along with many other passengers, I boarded to continue my journey.

But for some mysterious reason, the bus driver wouldn't start the bus or leave. The doors were open, and the brisk air flowed through the bus. After several minutes of waiting with no movement, someone asked if anyone knew why we were still stopped. A man said, "I know Turkish; let me ask the driver." He spoke to the driver, who then began shouting loudly. When passengers asked what was happening, what's wrong? The Iranian man explained that because this bus was an upgraded model, we had to pay an extra $20 per person, or the driver will not depart. We argued back, "We had already paid for our tickets in Tehran and that this connecting bus was included in that fare." We emphasized that it wasn't our fault and that we didn't request an upgrade. The man was asked to tell the driver to start the bus since it was getting very late. But when he relayed our message, the driver angrily screamed back and stormed off the bus. Then, another passenger suggested that we all just pay the extra fee so we could finally leave. He handed the money to the interpreter, and naturally, everyone followed suit. Only then did the driver come back and the bus finally left the station.

I traveled across Turkey, and a day and a half later I arrived in Istanbul. There, I rented a motel room in a neighborhood crowded with Iranians. At the motel, I shared the story about the odd incident with the bus driver at the border. Others told me this was a common scam. The driver, the interpreter, and the first contributor of money all work together as part of a transportation mafia. They use this trick frequently to cheat naïve passengers. "Welcome to Turkey," they said, grudgingly.

Arriving in Turkey gave me a brief window of just 90 days on a tourist visa to decide my next move. Desperate for a way forward, I started searching for a smuggler who could get me to Europe. Sometime earlier, I had met an Iranian named Seyyed, who ran an import-export business in Istanbul. I found his business and approached him to see if he had any contacts who might know a smuggler. He introduced me to someone who claimed to have the right connections. Istanbul is full of these things.

When I spoke with this man, I learned that the cost to be smuggled out of Turkey to some Western European countries ranged from $6,000 to $8,000 US. I didn't have that kind of money. All I had totaled to only about $400, which was running out fast. So, I asked if he could help me find a job to save up and go later. He told me that working on a tourist visa was illegal. I replied, "So it's okay to smuggle me, but it's not okay to work a job on a tourist visa?" He answered, "It is what it is."

Frustrated, I went back to Seyyed for advice. He asked, "Why do you want to be smuggled to Europe?" I explained that I couldn't return to Iran because my life was in danger and briefly shared a little of my story with him. He said, "Before trying any dangerous schemes, there might be another way. If you're legitimate and your life is truly at risk, there's an office in the United Nations that helps people like you."

I found out some more information and made my way to the UNHCR's office in Ankara. There, they took some details about my circumstances and told me they would be in contact. I was then sent from the capital of Turkey to Nevşehir, Cappadocia. In this new town, I was required to report to the Police Department every weekday. The officials took my Iranian passport and scheduled a brief interview to gather basic information about who I was and why I had fled Iran. They made it very clear—if I failed to check in and missed three consecutive days, they would consider me gone, and my case would be closed.

So, until the moment I left Turkey, I went as required every day and signed my name in a book, along with all the others seeking refugee status.

Life In the Wilderness

I spent three difficult and lonely years in Turkey. Like Iran, Turkey is a majority-Muslim country, but its population follows the Sunni branch of Islam. In tourist-heavy cities and sites, there's a polished façade of peaceful, tolerant Islam. But in everyday life among the local people, a different reality emerges, one shaped by the ideology of the Muslim Brotherhood, a hardline sect within Sunni Islam.

As a refugee, I had no legal right to work In Turkey. The government viewed foreigners as a threat to local jobs, so employment for asylum seekers was strictly prohibited. But I had to survive. I took whatever jobs I could find; most of them were in construction, grueling, backbreaking labor with half of the fair pay. Being Iranian already made me a target for prejudice, but once the Turkish contractor learned my name was Mohamad—and that I had become a Christian—the mistreatment grew worse. He gave me the hardest, dirtiest jobs.

At one construction site, I had to carry 100-pound bags of cement and plaster up five flights of stairs on my back. The building had an elevator, so I tried to use it. But the foreman stopped me. "Uh-uh," he said, waving his finger. "You'll make the elevator dirty. Take the stairs."

On the way down, I had to haul bags filled with jagged chunks of broken concrete and shattered glass. The sharp edges tore through the bags and cut into my back. I was bleeding, exhausted, and humiliated—but I had no other choice.

While living in Turkey and working among the Turks, I learned their language. Sometimes I wished I never had because once I understood it, I could hear every insult they threw at me, day after day.

Despite the persecution, I came into contact with two Christian couples through a home church in Turkey. Both couples worked with refugees and had a dramatic impact on my life. Their support during my lowest point sustained me through a time I may not have endured by myself.

Three months after arriving in Nevşehir, I had my first interview with UN officials. It felt more like an intense interrogation than an interview. I was stuck with an interviewer and a translator in a room for at least four hours, and every movement I made was closely watched and analyzed. When it finally ended, they told me a decision would be made soon and instructed me to return home and wait.

As I stepped out of the UNHCR building, I had a lump in my throat. I managed to walk just a few steps before I squatted down on the sidewalk and burst into tears. The intensity, the pressure, the weight of everything, it was all too much for me to carry in that moment.

Hearing a positive response from the UN was the thin thread of hope that kept me going through those harsh conditions. But that hope was shattered one evening after a long, exhausting day of construction. I came home, covered in dust and sweat, and as I did every evening, I pulled up the UNHCR website and typed in my case number. By this time, eight months had passed since my interview.

That day, the one word I feared stared back at me in bold red letters: REJECTED.

My head dropped, and I didn't have the strength to lift it again. The thought of being sent back to Iran crushed me. The idea of facing my father and hearing him say, "You failed again," was more than I could bear. I would rather die than face that shame.

My body broke under the weight of it all. I lay down on my metal bed—just a frame with worn springs and a crumbling mattress—and began to sweat and shake uncontrollably. The trembling was so violent you could hear the screws rattling loose beneath me. When I went to the bathroom, I passed blood for two days. I was tormented by thoughts of failure, by the uncertainty of what my future held.

But after a few days of silence, pain, and despair, something inside me stirred. I realized I had no choice but to keep going.

I was allowed to file a one-time appeal, which meant requesting a second interview. This was my last chance with the UN. When I submitted the appeal, I asked for the reason behind the initial rejection. Their response was disheartening. They said that as a new Christian, I seemed to have too much knowledge of the Bible. To them, it looked like I had been coached for the interview.

I was back to square one, facing the entire process again, fully aware this was my final opportunity. So, my stay in Turkey extended for two more long years.

Four months later, I was called in for my second interview. The interview was tough once again, this time with a different team. I repeated my story and presented all the documentation. The interviewer seemed cold and not impressed, but I laid everything out there honestly and openly.

Five days later, I heard back from them. This time, it was completely different—I was accepted. My case was approved. I was officially recognized as a religious refugee. I felt weightless, I could fly, even though I had no wings.

To Freedom

The day my refugee case finally moved forward was unforgettable, I had a departure date. This happened while I was part of a worship team attending a Christian conference. At dinner time, while everyone else was eating and fellowshipping, I felt a strong urge to go and check my case status online. I typed my case number into the UNHCR's website and saw that my case had been approved for resettlement in the United States, with flight dates already set. I jumped up, screamed with joy, and ran down the stairs to share the good news with my fellow believers. As I hurried down the steep stairs, I twisted my ankle, fell violently, rolled the rest of the way down, and crashed into the guard rail with a loud thud. Everyone rushed over to see what had happened. Despite the pain and screaming from my sprained ankle, I told them, "My case was accepted. All the long waiting is over. I'm going to America."

I was rushed straight to the hospital that evening. My ankle had swollen like a balloon. After several morphine injections, X-rays, and a full examination, the doctor told me it needed to be set in a cast. I would be on crutches for a while. But as I hobbled out of the hospital, I couldn't have cared less. I was going to America. Nothing could stop me, even with a busted ankle, I was walking (well, hobbling) into freedom.

SECTION FOUR
Refuge

My trip to America was surreal. I could hardly believe it was really happening. On the plane, I actually had to pinch myself because I kept thinking I was just dreaming, the dream of leaving behind the suffocating oppression of the Islamic society, the discrimination and hardship of Turkey, and the control of the Islamic culture.

It started with an eleven-hour bus ride from Nevşehir to Istanbul. I spent the night at the airport, afraid of being late or missing my flight. That night in the airport, I cut off my cast, threw away my crutches, and dragged my foot across the airport floor to reach my gate. One suitcase and the clothes on my back held everything I owned. From Istanbul, I had a fourteen-hour direct flight to Los Angeles. When I landed, it took five hours just to clear customs. After that, I gathered my one bag—my entire life—and walked from the international terminal to the domestic terminal for a final six-hour flight to Seattle.

This was the city UNHCR had allocated me to go to. My missionary friends who lived in Turkey were acquainted with a

Forsaking My Father's Religion

Korean Church in Seattle and introduced me to them, and so this is where I started my life in the U.S.

When I Get to The U.S., It's Gonna Be Easy!
Everything in America felt enormous. The first thing I noticed was the sheer size of everything. I felt like a tiny ant in a land made for giants. On the drive from the airport to my apartment, the roads looked like airport runways, with so many lanes, so wide, and cars the size of small buildings. I wasn't crammed into a claustrophobic taxi with six other people, either. Here, everyone had personal space, something I didn't know was possible in a moving vehicle or shops.

America is vast. The streets stretched endlessly, the buildings looked like movie sets, and even the grocery stores felt like football fields. It was overwhelming in a strangely impressive way.

My first month in the U.S. was rough. I was battling homesickness, culture shock, and depression. Everything was foreign, especially the food. And the gray, rainy skies of Seattle didn't help. The weather was as confused as I was, drizzling for hours without ever really deciding to rain properly.

One day, I ventured into a grocery store. I needed to eat. What should've been a five-minute errand turned into a two-hour expedition. I was just trying to buy a simple snack, but I stood frozen in front of a wall of chips that looked more like an art exhibit. There were endless choices: baked, fried, kettle-cooked, gluten-free, organic, low-sodium, extra spicy, no-spice, lime-flavored, and chips identifying as vegetables. I didn't know if I was shopping or taking a personality test.

On my way home, holding my precious bag of overpriced confusion, I passed a very large man sitting on the sidewalk. Suddenly, he shouted, "CHANGE!" I jumped, startled, thinking, Change what? My clothes? My attitude? My religion? My entire life? I walked away quickly and swore I'd never take that route again. Later, when I told someone about it, they laughed and said, "He was just a poor beggar asking for coins. He wasn't yelling at you." Where I come from, poor people are not fat! It was both a relief and a lesson—America spoke English, but not always the kind I understood.

A few days later, my caseworker arrived to process some of my paperwork. I asked if it would be possible to move to a different city. He seemed pleased and immediately offered to send my documentation to the destination of my choice—one less case on his workload. I chose Los Angeles, home to the largest population of Iranians outside of Iran.

L.A. Where You Meet the Angels

When I arrived in Los Angeles, the culture shock hit me again, this time in an unexpected way. It felt like I had traveled not just across the world but also back in time. The Iranian community in Los Angeles, many of whom had left Iran during the 1979 Revolution, had preserved their customs, traditions, and language like museum artifacts. During a drive through the San Fernando Valley, I was stunned. I saw more Farsi signs for shops, businesses, and restaurants than I had probably seen in Iran itself. I thought to myself, how is this even possible? And how is it allowed? It felt like I had stepped into a Persian mini nation inside America. That's when I learned the nickname locals had given it—Tehrangeles. And honestly, it made perfect sense why they call it that. The Farsi the local Iranian community spoke was so formal and old-fashioned that it felt like I was wading through classical Persian poetry just to follow along.

Weeks later, I landed a job at a Persian restaurant. At first, it seemed simple, I was just a waiter. But when the weekend came, the place transformed. The lights dimmed, the music cranked up, belly dancers took the floor, and the air filled with the smell of alcohol and smoke. It wasn't a restaurant anymore; it was a nightclub. Nothing about the business was official. No contracts, no payroll, no insurance. Everything ran on cash, completely off the books. One night, as I stood there holding a shot tray in the middle of the chaos, I asked myself, "Did I really escape persecution, cross borders, nearly starve, just to end up in a place that feels like an underground third-world cabaret?"

There was nothing positive, uplifting, or spiritual about that place. I was a believer—I needed to be connected to a fellowship. "God," I prayed, "please lead me to other Christians." I was spiritually starving again. I needed a lifeline fast.

One day, a friend invited me to a small bilingual church just a couple of blocks from where I lived. I went. That little church became my rescue boat. It was like stepping into the light after walking through a long, thick fog. I was encouraged, restored, and reminded of why I had come to America in the first place.

As only God could have planned, that's where I met the angel who would later become my wife. A year after we met, we were married. My journey had taken me from persecution and rejection to love and belonging. God was not just rescuing me. He was rebuilding my life.

Meeting my beautiful wife and getting married to her was a life-changing experience for me. But nothing can compare to the life-changing experience of accepting Jesus as my Lord and Savior. By accepting Him into my life and converting to Christianity, nothing changed on the outside. I have had to face a new chapter of challenges, including a life-threatening one. But inside me, there is something new; the spirit man was reconciled to God, alive, and full of hope and joy.

My life now has meaning and purpose, something I received directly from the Lord Himself while reading my Bible. One day, during my daily reading, I came to the Gospel of Mark chapter 5. It tells the story of a man possessed by a legion of demons. The Bible says he lived among the tombs. No one could bind him, not even with chains. Night and day, his dwelling place was the graveyards, crying out and cutting himself with stones. His life was consumed by torment and isolation.

But everything changed when he encountered Jesus.

With just a word, Jesus set him free. The man was completely healed—restored in his right mind. Then, in verse 18, it says, "And when Jesus got into the boat, he who had been demon-possessed begged Him that he might be with Him. However,

Jesus did not permit him, but said to him, 'Go home to your friends and tell them what great things the Lord has done for you, and how He has had compassion on you.'" The man actually obeyed and did exactly what Jesus commanded him to do. When people heard what he had to say, they marveled.

His story wasn't just something I read—it was a mirror. I saw myself in Mark chapter 5. I was that tormented man, chained, crying, cutting myself, and living among tombs. And then Jesus came. He delivered me. He spoke those exact words to me when I wanted to follow Him, and I knew they were mine: "Go and tell people what I have done for you!"

I obeyed, and if you are reading this book, if you're being moved or marveling at what God has done for me, it's because I obeyed what He has commanded me to do. And YES, he has been so good to me.

SECTION FIVE

Your Decision

After reading the story of my life, you may ask yourself, "Is the Truth worth dying for?"

Leaving Islam or even speaking about it is very costly; however, thousands upon thousands of Muslims are willing to accept the truth and lay down their lives for it. Would you be willing to accept the Truth and stand by it?

Jesus said, "I am the way, the truth, and the life: no man comes to the Father, but by me." John 14:6

The Word of God promises, "That if you confess with your mouth the Lord Jesus and believe in your heart that God has raised Him from the dead, you will be saved. For with the heart, one believes unto righteousness, and with the mouth confession is made unto salvation." Romans 10:9-10 Romans 10:13 says, "Whoever calls on the name of the LORD shall be saved."

God, through His grace, has already provided forgiveness for our sins. All you need to do is simply believe and receive it. Pray out loud, "God, I confess Jesus as my Lord and my

Savior. I believe that You raised Him from the dead, and I receive my salvation. Thank you for rescuing me!"

The very moment you commit your life to Jesus Christ; the truth of His Word instantly comes to pass in your spirit. This is the part of you that becomes brand new. I want to encourage you to get a Bible and begin to read it. Let the truth of God's Word renew your mind. Romans 12:2

Share this message with someone. It is easy for your name to appear in someone's testimonial. Changing the destination of their life and their generations to come. Someone did that for me; his name is Rasoul. Let's share the good news and impact the world around us. **OR YOU CAN ALSO HELP US GET THE GOOD NEWS OUT TO MUSLIMS.**

The purpose of this book is to share the Good News of the Gospel, offer hope to the hopeless, and raise awareness about what the religion of Islam can do to its followers. 100% of the proceeds from this book go directly to the ministry of Engaging Muslims with Christ.

For information, write or email us at:

Iranian Christians International
P.O. Box 50007, Colorado Springs, CO 80949
ICI@IranChristians.org
IranChristians.org

To hear more testimonies of Ex-Muslims like Mohamad's and learn how to evangelize Muslims, visit the ministry's YouTube channel.
youtube.com/MohamadFaridi